W9-BFC-826

GREAT AMERICAN MEMORIALS

REMEMBERING KOREA

THE KOREAN WAR VETERANS MEMORIAL

Brent Ashabranner

Photographs by
Jennifer Ashabranner

Twenty-First Century Books • Brookfield, Connecticut

Photographs courtesy of U.S. Army Corps of Engineers: p. 7; U.S. Army: pp. 23, 26, 28, 31; U.S. Marine Corps: p. 24, 30.
All other photographs are by Jennifer Ashabranner.

Published by Twenty-First Century Books
A Division of The Millbrook Press, Inc.
2 Old New Milford Road
Brookfield, Connecticut 06804
www.millbrookpress.com

Copyright © 2001 by Brent Ashabranner
Photographs copyright © 2001 by Jennifer Ashabranner
All rights reserved
Printed in the United States of America
5 4 3 2 1

Library of Congress Cataloging-in-Publication Data
Ashabranner, Brent K., 1921–
Remembering Korea: the Korean War Veterans Memorial/
Brent Ashabranner; photographs by Jennifer Ashabranner.
p. cm.—(Great American memorials)
Includes bibliographical references and index.
ISBN 0–7613–2156–X (lib. bdg.)
1. Korean War Veterans Memorial (Washington, D.C.)
2. Korean War, 1950–1953. I. Ashabranner, Jennifer, ill. II. Title.

DS921.92.U6 A84 2001
951.904'26—dc21   00–068282

CONTENTS

1

A DAY TO REMEMBER

THEY ARE larger than life, but they seem alive. They are made of unpolished stainless steel, but you can almost feel their living flesh and sense the blood pounding in their veins. They are nineteen in number, a column of American soldiers emerging warily from a grove of trees. Their weapons are at the ready as they climb a hill where unseen dangers lurk.

The patrol is a part, the most dramatic part, of the Korean War Veterans Memorial. An American flag, toward which the patrol is advancing, is also a part of the memorial, as is a pool of gently flowing water—a "Pool of Remembrance"—behind the flag. A black

5

THE LEAD SCOUT *moves resolutely forward, his M-1 rifle at his side.*

A BIRD'S EYE VIEW *of the Korean War Veterans Memorial shows the relationship of its main features.*

granite wall to the right of the patrol completes the memorial. Into the highly polished panels of the wall are etched the images of more than 2,400 servicemen and -women. They represent the hundreds of thousands who supported the ground troops and helped fight the war in Korea: nurses, doctors, ambulance drivers, rescue helicopter pilots, airplane mechanics, a war dog, and scores of others.

The Korean War Veterans Memorial, located in an area of grass and trees on the National Mall in Washington, DC, was dedicated on July 27, 1995. It completes a triad of memorials at the western end of the Mall. The other memorials in the grouping are the majestic Lincoln Memorial and the unforgettable black wall of names that is the Vietnam Veterans Memorial. The Korean War Veterans Memorial takes its place with them in the heart of American history.

THE PATH FROM *the Lincoln Memorial brings visitors into immediate contact with the patrol. The granite strips over which the patrol is moving are symbolic of the obstacles of war that the soldiers had to overcome.*

On a summer day in 2000, the 25th of June, Jennifer and I went early to the Korean War Veterans Memorial. Although it was not yet eight o'clock, many people were at the memorial, and I knew that the number would increase steadily as the day progressed. For this day marked a moment in history that had affected millions of American lives. On a summer day such as this—June 25, 1950—Communist army forces from the north had invaded South Korea, and the Korean War had begun. The bitter struggle to contain the spread of communism in Asia lasted three years and cost 37,000 American lives.

At this memorial built to honor Korean War veterans, a ceremony was held to commemorate the fiftieth anniversary of the beginning of that war. Veterans of the war from all over the country had come to Washington for the commemoration. One of them was Wilfred Bauman, an Army 25th Infantry Division veteran, who drove from Duanesburg, New York, and was at the memorial early. He probably spoke for most veterans when he told a *Washington Post* reporter: "There's only one fiftieth anniversary, and I wanted to be here for it."

Half a century is a long time. Most of the veterans at the memorial on this day were in their late teens and early twenties when they had fought in Korea. Some had also served in World War II. Now they were in their late sixties and seventies. Many veterans were there with their wives and some with their now middle-aged children. A sprinkling of grandchildren stretched the memorial visitors to three generations.

From their reactions I could tell that most of those at the memorial were seeing it for the first time. They were drawn almost magnetically to the scouting patrol and caught immediately in its power. Suddenly, you are there, a part of the group. You can feel the danger the soldiers feel. One of them has turned his head sharply at some sound and signals others to beware. They all stare intently in different directions as they move through the rough terrain. A soldier near the front of the patrol grips his radio, his walkie-talkie, tightly as his eyes probe what lies ahead. The lead scout pushes resolutely ahead, his weapon at his side.

A SIGNAL CORPS SCOUT *stares intently at some sign of danger. The sense of movement in the sculptures is superb.*

A man I was standing near pointed to the rifle that the lead scout was carrying and said to his wife, "That's an M-1. I carried one all over Korea."

The wall, too, was receiving its share of attention. Veterans walked along it slowly, trying to find wartime activities they had been a part of, perhaps looking for the face of someone they had known. The engraved images of people, equipment, and activities were taken from Korean War photographs in the National Archives

THE MEMORIAL'S BLACK GRANITE *wall contains more than 2,400 photographic etchings symbolizing the vast effort that sustained the foot troops, including nurses, chaplains, airmen, gunners, mechanics, cooks, and Canine Corps, among others.*

and National Air and Space Museum collections in Washington. Name tags and unit insignia were removed before the engravings of service people were made, but sharp-eyed veterans are almost always sure they have found a picture of someone they knew during the war.

Throughout the morning people paused at the Pool of Remembrance. Highly reflective black granite from Canada forms the base of the pool, which is 30 feet (9 meters) in diameter. Water

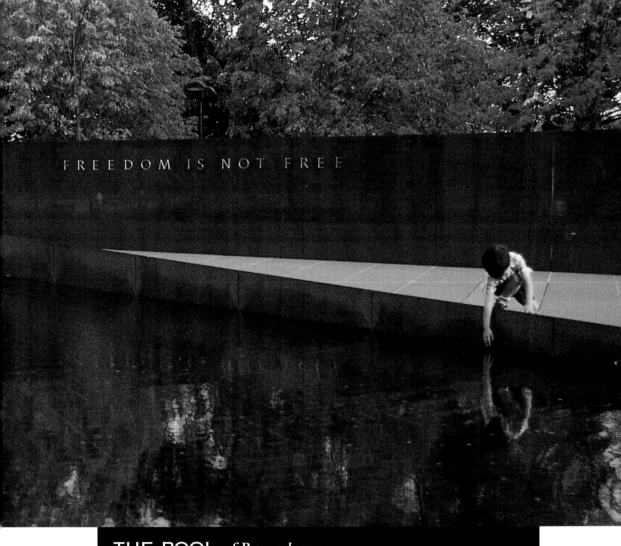

THE POOL *of Remembrance.*

circulates continuously, but the surface is smooth, glasslike, and invites quiet reflection on the sacrifices made by Americans in Korea. A low black granite wall that slices into the pool has no pictures of servicemen and -women on it, but high on the wall the words FREEDOM IS NOT FREE are engraved.

From the first time I saw it, that terse sentence summed up for me the meaning of the Korean War Veterans Memorial. The freedom of South Korea had been won at a high price. The triumph of America over communism during the Cold War decades had been won at a high price. The memorial's wary, heavily burdened foot soldiers; the thousands of people and support activities portrayed on the black granite wall; the Pool of Remembrance for all those who died in battle tell the story of that price. Freedom is not free.

The commemoration ceremony started at four o'clock. By that time more than seven thousand veterans, their families, and others interested in the commemoration were seated in folding chairs around a stage that had been set up near the memorial. A number of Koreans were in the audience, both Korean Americans and visitors from Korea.

As the crowd settled in, several groups provided pre-ceremony entertainment—a Korean dance group, the Coast Guard Dixieland Band, the United States Marine Drum and Bugle Corps, and the United States Air Force Band. The Air Force Singing Sergeants added a touch of nostalgia with "Those Nifty Fifties" songs such as "Mr. Sandman, Bring Me a Dream" and "How Much Is That Doggie in the Window?" The hot afternoon sun burned down from a cloudless sky, and the audience was grateful for the bottles of cold water passed out by military volunteers.

The fiftieth anniversary commemoration was sponsored by the United States Department of Defense, and Secretary of Defense William S. Cohen hosted the ceremony. After the presentation of colors, Secretary Cohen called on Ambassador Kong-Hoo Lee of the Republic of Korea to speak. The ambassador thanked the United States for leading the United Nations (UN) forces in saving his country from the Communist invasion fifty years ago. The Republic of Korea was now America's eighth-largest trading partner, the ambassador said, and more than a million Koreans and Americans visited each other's country every year.

What if America had lost the Cold War in Asia? the ambassador asked.

The next speaker was former Senator John Glenn. The first American to be put into an orbital spaceflight (1962), Colonel Glenn had been a fighter pilot with the U.S. Marine Corps during the Korean War. As a senator, Glenn had been a strong supporter of the proposal for a Korean War Veterans Memorial, reminding his fellow senators that the purpose of memorials is to keep memory alive. In his remarks on this day, he remembered. "Coming in the time shadow of World War II's huge global scope," Senator Glenn told the crowd, "Korea was small, but it was deadly." In addition to the thousands of Americans killed or wounded, more than eight thousand are still missing, their fates unknown.

The principal speaker at the commemoration ceremony was President Bill Clinton, and he was at his eloquent best. The presi-

PRESIDENT BILL CLINTON *speaking at the fiftieth anniversary ceremony marking the beginning of the Korean War.*

dent began with an indirect reference to the fact that the Korean War has often been called the Forgotten War. "All across our nation today," the president said, "our fellow citizens are coming together to say to men and women who fought for freedom half a century ago, half a world away, we will never forget your bravery, we will always honor your service and your sacrifice."

Mr. Clinton made a special point of the fact that until 1999 Congress had called the war a "conflict," not a war. "Korea was war at its worst," he said, "but it was America at its best. . . . Korea was not a police action or a crisis or a clash. It was a war; a hard brutal war. And the men and women who fought it were heroes."

The president told the audience that in 1950 the leaders of the Communist nations did not believe that America would stand up for South Korea. America didn't want another war. The blood hadn't dried on World War II. But America did stand up and drew "a line in the sand on the Cold War."

"I submit to you today," Mr. Clinton said, "that looking back through the long lens of history, it is clear that the stand America took in Korea was indispensable to our ultimate victory in the Cold War. Because we stood our ground in Korea, the Soviet Union drew a clear lesson that America would fight for freedom."

Without the sacrifices that Americans made in Korea, the Cold War might have had a much different outcome, the president continued. And he said that "the line of history" can be drawn straight from the battlefields of Korea to the rejoicing young people who stood on the Berlin Wall in 1989 to witness the collapse of the Soviet Union.

President Clinton concluded his message by saying to all veterans of the Korean War: ". . . fifty years ago you helped make the world that we know today possible. You proved to all humanity just how good our nation can be at its best. You showed us, through your example, that freedom is not free, but it can be maintained. Today, your fellow Americans say: we remember and we are very grateful."

The commemoration ceremony ended with a flyover of Korean War–era aircraft: rescue helicopters; F-51 Mustangs; F-86

Sabres, the aircraft that produced many aces; B-26 bombers; C-47 cargo planes. The last planes to fly over were jets, one plane absent from the usual six-plane pattern. They were flying the traditional "Missing Man" formation in memory of comrades who had not returned to base.

At the end of the program hundreds of people streamed to the memorial, some returning for a second look, some for a first visit. Many posed for photographs in front of the wall. Others took pictures of wreaths and other mementos that had been placed at the

A WREATH *of remembrance.*

wall. I saw one veteran carrying a sign that said FORGOTTEN NO MORE.

My attention was drawn to a young boy who was studying one of the panels of the wall. "Uncle George!" he called after a bit. "It's a bunch of Seabees. You're here on the wall!"

A man I took to be Uncle George, a campaign cap covering most of his gray hair, bent down to look at the wall. "I don't think so," he said.

"It is you," the boy insisted.

Uncle George kept looking. "Well," he said at last. "I guess it could be. Except I never was that young."

2

THE KOREAN WAR

KOREA is an East Asian peninsular country 600 miles (966 kilometers) long and only 160 miles (257 kilometers) wide at its narrowest point close to the 38th parallel. It is bounded by the Yellow Sea in the west, the Sea of Japan in the east, and the Korea Strait in the south. Its land boundary in the north is primarily with China and a short distance with Russia. The great Yalu and Tumen rivers form the northern border. With an area of 85,049 square miles (220,277 square kilometers), Korea is about one-third larger than the state of Florida and has a somewhat similar shape.

Korea is an ancient civilization. During the first six centuries A.D. three separate kingdoms emerged. Although politically separate, they were related ethnically and linguistically. Over the centuries they fought each other and sometimes united to resist Chinese or Mongol invasions. There were long periods of warfare and other periods of peace and great cultural development in the arts: painting, ceramics, music, literature. The world's first movable metal type was invented in Korea in 1234, preceding that of Gutenberg by two centuries.

Throughout the centuries, Korea wanted fiercely to be left alone by the outside world. In fact, Korea has been called the "hermit kingdom" because of its unyielding opposition in the nineteenth century to Western efforts—particularly by France, Germany, and the United States—to promote diplomatic and trade relations.

How then did it happen that in 1950 the United States was drawn into a bitter war in that small, remote Asian country that few Americans knew anything about?

The answer has its roots in the emergence of Japan as a world power. During the latter part of the nineteenth century, Japan began an imperial expansion in East Asia and was victorious in wars against both China and Russia for control of the Korean peninsula and other parts of East Asia. In 1910, Japan annexed Korea, officially declaring it to be a part of Japan.

Japan did not stop there. Determined to be dominant in Asia and the Pacific, the Japanese formed a military alliance with Germany and Italy in World War II and began hostilities against the United States at Pearl Harbor, Hawaii, in 1941. In a devastating war, the United States joined its major allies, Great Britain and the Soviet Union, in fighting Germany and Italy in Europe. The United States fought fierce battles against the Japanese army and navy throughout the Pacific. Following the dropping of atomic bombs on the Japanese cities of Hiroshima and Nagasaki by the United States, Japan surrendered in August 1945 and was occupied by U.S. forces.

In a move to strip Japan of its territorial conquests, the victorious allies agreed that Korean independence should be restored. A trusteeship was established, with the United States occupying the southern half of Korea, the Soviet Union the northern half. The division was made at Korea's 38th parallel. The purpose of the trusteeship was to create stable conditions in which Koreans could set up their own independent government.

Shortly after World War II ended, however, a deep division arose between the Communist Soviet Union and the democratic countries of Western Europe and the United States. In 1946, Joseph Stalin, the iron-fisted dictator of the Soviet Union, declared that international peace was impossible "under the present capitalist development of the world economy."

In response to this Soviet threat, President Harry Truman announced that "it must be the policy of the United States to support free peoples who are resisting attempted subjugation by armed minorities or by outside pressures."

The Cold War had begun.

The United States asked the newly created United Nations to supervise elections throughout Korea to give the Korean people a chance to elect a new national government. The Soviets, however, refused to permit the United Nations to hold elections in North Korea.

South Koreans voted in a UN-supervised election that selected a National Assembly. The assembly approved the country's constitution, and the Republic of Korea was formally established on August 14, 1948. The Republic of Korea occupied the southern half of the Korean peninsula below the 38th parallel.

A few months later, North Korea held its own election, which was carried out under tight Soviet control. The Communist party came into power and established the Democratic People's Republic of Korea. The new country occupied all of the Korean peninsula north of the 38th parallel.

With the creation of the Republic of Korea, the United States ended it occupation of South Korea. Only a few hundred American officers and enlisted personnel remained to continue training South Korea's small, lightly armed security forces. The South Korean army was intended only to help preserve domestic order and defend the border against minor incursions.

The Soviets, too, withdrew their occupation troops from North Korea after the election there. But during their occupation they had trained a large North Korean army and equipped it with heavy tanks and long-range artillery. Although the United States did not anticipate a major North Korean attack, the clear Soviet intention was to leave a North Korean army capable of crushing South Korea and unifying the peninsula under a Communist government.

The Korean War began with a surprise attack on June 25, 1950. Eight divisions of the North Korean army, numbering 90,000 soldiers, and an armored brigade crossed the 38th parallel and invaded South Korea. The invaders drove straight for South Korea's capital, Seoul, which is near the 38th parallel. The Soviet Union provided technical military advisors and logistical support for the invasion.

In New York, the UN Security Council met in emergency session as soon as news of the invasion reached it. The council quickly passed a resolution calling for an immediate end to the hostilities and withdrawal of North Korean forces to the 38th parallel. The Soviet member of the Security Council was absent because of a Soviet boycott protesting the United Nations' refusal to seat Communist China's representative. Had the Soviet representative been present at the meeting, he could have vetoed the resolution and doubtless would have.

Created only five years earlier, in 1945, to maintain international peace and security and promote cooperation in solving humanitarian problems, the young United Nations faced its first grave crisis.

In those late June days, President Harry Truman also faced some difficult decisions. He strongly believed that America had to support the United Nations. "It was our idea," Truman said, referring to the establishment of the new international organization. "In this first big test we just can't let them down." Truman ordered the evacuation of American civilians in Korea and the shipment of arms and supplies to South Korea.

On June 26, General Douglas MacArthur, commander of the American occupation forces in Japan, reported that the South Korean army was incapable of stopping the Communist onslaught. That night President Truman met with his top military advisors and approved air and naval support for the forces of South Korea. Use of American ground troops in Korea was not authorized.

On June 27 the Republic of Korea appealed to the UN for help. The Soviet member was still absent, and without hesitation the Security Council recommended that United Nations members furnish assistance to South Korea to "repel the armed attack and to restore international peace and security to the area." Fifty-three member nations approved the Security Council's recommendation.

Conditions in South Korea worsened by the hour. On June 29, Communist forces captured Seoul. Once more President Truman assembled his staff. He was given the grim news that there was no hope of stopping the North Korean army with air and sea power alone. The president did not hesitate. He authorized the use of American ground troops in Korea. The U.S. Congress supported President Truman's decision.

The United Nations asked the United States to lead the Unified Command to stop North Korean aggression. The United States accepted the responsibility, and President Truman appointed General Douglas MacArthur as commanding general of all UN forces.

During the course of the war, twenty-two nations—including the United States and the Republic of Korea—contributed to the United Nations military effort in Korea. A British Commonwealth division had contingents from Australia, Canada, India, New Zealand, South Africa, and the United Kingdom. Turkey sent a full brigade. Belgium, Colombia, Ethiopia, France, Greece, the Netherlands, the Philippines, and Thailand sent infantry battalions. The tiny country of Luxembourg sent an infantry company. Denmark, Italy, Norway, and Sweden provided medical services. Several of these countries gave naval and air support. While this international military contribution was extremely important and expressed strong disapproval of North Korean aggression, the main burden of fighting fell upon South Korea and the United States.

When the fighting in Korea began, the United States was poorly prepared to wage war. After World War II, public sentiment was strongly against maintaining a large standing military establishment. By 1950, U.S. military strength had become dangerously weak. In 1945 there were 12 million men and women in uniform; by 1948 there were only 1.5 million, and no one had been drafted since 1947. With heavy commitments in postwar Europe and Asia, the U.S. military was spread very thin.

But ready or not, Americans were again called to action.

The ground troops most readily available to General MacArthur included the 1st Cavalry Division and the 7th, 24th, and 25th Infantry divisions, all a part of the U.S. Eighth Army, headquartered in Japan as the army of occupation. But those units had received limited combat training, and many were well below their designated strength. Most of their equipment was left over from World War II and seriously out-of-date.

General MacArthur assigned command of U.S. Eighth Army forces in Korea to Lieutenant General Walton H. Walker. Nicknamed Bulldog, Walker was a highly experienced officer who had commanded a machine-gun company in World War I and had served as one of General George Patton's corps commanders in World War II. At the request of Republic of Korea President Syngman Rhee, Walker also assumed command of the South Korean army.

After capturing Seoul, the North Korean army pushed relentlessly south, intent on taking over the entire Korean peninsula. The first U.S. combat troops arrived in Korea on July 1, disembarked in the port city of Pusan, and quickly moved north. One of the newly arrived units was the 1st Battalion, 21st Infantry Regiment of the Eighth Army's 24th Division. In an effort to delay the North Korean army's advance, the 1st Battalion was ordered to take a defensive position astride the main road near Osan, a city about 30 miles (48 kilometers) south of Seoul. Named Task Force Smith for its commander, Lieutenant Colonel Charles "Brad" Smith, this battalion, with a strength of 540 men, would be the first American combat unit to go face-to-face with the enemy. The day was July 5.

The Americans dug foxholes on both sides of the road and waited in the rain for the North Koreans. They did not have long

ON JULY 18, 1950, *men of the 24th Infantry Regiment prepare to move toward the front.*

to wait. Soon a column of fearsome Soviet-made T-34 tanks, thirty-three of them, appeared on the horizon and rumbled down the highway. The tanks were followed by a long line of trucks loaded with North Korean infantry.

The ill-prepared Americans fired bazookas, but the 2.36 rockets bounced harmlessly off the tanks. Second Lieutenant Carl Bernard was there that day. He remembers taking a bazooka from his men and firing it with the same result. "They didn't hurt the tanks," he said. "The piece-of-trash bazookas we were carrying didn't do anything but annoy the tankers."

And Bernard has other grim memories: "I lost a lot of people who I wouldn't have lost if we had been better equipped and better prepared. We had machine guns that didn't work. We had radios that didn't work."

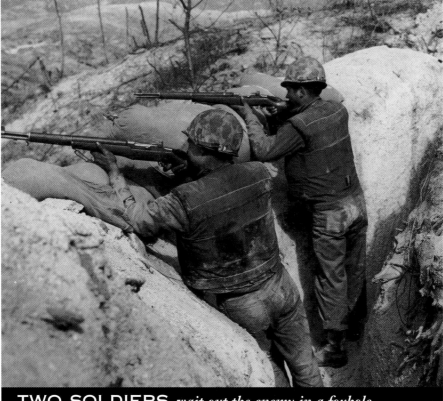

TWO SOLDIERS *wait out the enemy in a foxhole.*

Task Force Smith put up a fight against the overwhelming power and numbers of the North Koreans and held out for several hours before they were completely outflanked. Realizing the hopelessness of their position, Smith ordered a withdrawal. Casualties in the disorganized retreat were heavy; almost two hundred Americans were killed, wounded, or missing in the delaying action that did not work.

In those early days of July, U.S. Eighth Army forces continued to arrive at Pusan and moved quickly to Taejon, a city about halfway between Seoul and Pusan. With the loss of Seoul to the North Koreans, Taejon had become the temporary capital of South Korea and a target toward which the North Korean army was driving. Two weeks of bitter fighting between the North Koreans and the U.S. troops ended with North Korea's superior numbers and firepower forcing the Americans to retreat. But despite heavy losses, the Eighth Army units had done their job, delaying the southward advance of the North Koreans for a crucial half month. In that time thousands more U.S. combat troops had reached Pusan.

But by early August the Eighth Army had been pushed deep into southeastern Korea and held only a small portion of the peninsula around Pusan. The loss of that vital port could well have meant the loss of the war. General Walker ordered a stand along a 140-mile (225-kilometer) line that arched from the Korea Strait to the Sea of Japan and protected Pusan. American divisions defended the western segment of the line, known as the Pusan Perimeter, and South Korean troops defended the northern segment.

Some of the bitterest fighting of the war took place along the Pusan Perimeter. In those August and early September days, thousands of U.S. and South Korean soldiers died, but they inflicted much heavier losses on the North Koreans. On August 8, the North Korean army breached the perimeter line at the Naktong River. The inexperienced but fiercely determined U.S. troops fought back and repelled the attacks. During that time, the U.S. Eighth Army was strengthened by the arrival of the 5th Regimental Combat Team from Hawaii, an infantry division from the United States, and

A LOOKOUT *from the 5th Regimental Combat Team takes a moment to rest.*

a British infantry brigade. By mid-September, the UN forces had secured the Pusan Perimeter.

With much of the North Korean army deeply engaged in the southern part of the peninsula, General MacArthur ordered a dangerous but brilliant amphibious assault near the Yellow Sea city of Inchon, only a few miles from Seoul. Tidal conditions allowed only a short time for reaching the beach, but on September 15 the 1st Marine Division and the 7th Infantry Division stormed ashore successfully and were joined by several thousand South Korean recruits. The attack caught the North Korean army completely by surprise, and the landings were only lightly opposed. In five days of skillful maneuvering, the UN forces reached the outskirts of Seoul. After a week of arduous street-to-street fighting, the North Korean army was driven out of the capital city. On September 29, Seoul was returned to President Rhee.

Strengthened UN forces in the south now took the offensive beyond the Pusan Perimeter. Reeling from the defeat at Seoul, the North Korean army was soon in complete disarray and retreated north of the 38th parallel.

The UN General Assembly called for the restoration of peace and security throughout Korea and authorized UN forces to enter North Korea. American and South Korean troops advanced rapidly northward. On October 19, the U.S. Eighth Army captured Pyong-yang, the North Korean capital. UN Command forces moved toward Korea's Yalu River border with China to complete UN control of the entire country. MacArthur predicted that American troops might be home by Christmas.

But then the war in Korea took a disastrous turn for the United Nations. In 1949 the Chinese Communists had emerged victorious from a two-decades-long civil war against Chiang Kai-Shek and his nationalist Kuomintang party. Now, in 1950, with a huge standing army, Mao Tse-tung, chairman of the ruling Communist party in China, made a decision to rescue Communist North Korea and thereby assure China of a Communist neighbor on its border.

In the hills and mountains beyond the Yalu River, Chinese military forces had been quietly gathering for months. American military intelligence had some knowledge of this buildup but no idea of its true size. General MacArthur and most of his advisors believed that China would not enter the war.

That mistaken belief ended abruptly in late October when Chinese troops crossed the Yalu River in massive force. On October 25 they surprised Republic of Korea troops near the Yalu River with deadly effect. In early November the Chinese attacked the U.S. Eighth Army in three different places in the northeast, forcing

MEN FROM THE *2nd Infantry Division north of the Chongchon River keep watch for Communist-led North Korean troops in November 1950.*

the Americans to retreat. As winter approached the number of Chinese troops in Korea grew to 300,000. North Korean units were reassembling to fight under Chinese leadership.

On November 27, Chinese forces trapped the 1st Marine Division and elements of the Eighth Army in the Changjin (Chosin) Reservoir, the site of an important hydroelectric plant in central North Korea. Eight Chinese divisions charged down from the surrounding mountains intent on completely destroying the Americans. There followed four weeks of intensely fierce warfare, during which the U.S. Marines and Army completed a successful fighting withdrawal through 78 miles (125 kilometers) of mountain roads to an east coast port. From there they were evacuated by the U.S. Navy. American forces suffered 9,000 casualties, the Chinese an estimated 25,000.

During the fighting at and retreat from Changjin Reservoir, winter came to Korea and left hundreds, even thousands, of the U.S. fighters with severe frostbite. The war in Korea would last through three winters, and veterans of the war say, almost without exception, that there were two enemies: the Chinese and the weather. In the hills and mountains of the country, the cold was merciless, temperatures dropping sometimes to -20°F (-6.67°C) or below. Weapons froze. Food froze. Skin cracked and blood oozed out. Men lost fingers and toes and died of frostbite. The cold numbed the senses, froze the fighting spirit.

And yet the UN forces found the spirit to fight. They were pushed back to the 38th parallel and tried to make a stand there. The Chinese pressure was too great, and the UN divisions withdrew deeper into South Korea. In January of the new year, 1951, Seoul was captured again by the Communists.

The UN forces regrouped, replaced their combat losses, and began once more to fight their way north. Operations Thunderbolt, Killer, Ripper, and Rugged carried the UN forces forward. They advanced slowly and methodically, ridge by ridge, wiping out each pocket of resistance before moving on. In mid-March the Eighth Army liberated Seoul and reached the 38th parallel once more.

In June 1951, with the battle lines now set along the preinvasion boundary, the Soviet delegate to the United Nations proposed negotiations to end armed hostilities. Both sides agreed to negotiate. Peace talks dragged on for two years. They were often bitter, bad-tempered, harsh. The battlefield stalemate of those years was often interrupted by artillery duels, ambushes, raids, and costly battles with such names as Bloody Ridge, Heartbreak Ridge, Pork Chop Hill, and Old Baldy.

IN SEPTEMBER 1951, *men of the 1ˢᵗ Marine Division rest after killing an enemy sniper hiding in a Korean hut.*

Finally, on July 27, 1953, a Military Armistice Agreement was signed at the village of Panmunjom near the 38th parallel. Both sides agreed to cease fighting. The two Koreas, North and South, remained divided by a Demilitarized Zone (DMZ) established on each side of the 38th parallel. The Korean War was over.

The Korean War had been fought at terrible cost. Almost 37,000 Americans had died in Korea; more than 103,000 had been wounded. Missing Americans numbered 8,100. More than 50,000 South Korean soldiers were killed, more than 350,000 were wounded. Casualties of other UN countries in the war exceeded 16,000, of which 3,000 were killed. Estimated enemy casualties

GRIEF FOR A LOST COMRADE *overwhelms an American soldier. In the background another soldier carefully fills out casualty tags.*

were more than 1,500,000, of whom 900,000 were Chinese. Civilian casualties are unknown but are estimated to be in the millions. South Korea was heavily damaged by enemy shelling. North Korea was in ruins from U.S. Air Force bombs. Railroads were destroyed, bridges down, tunnels blocked, highways full of craters, ports in shambles, buildings gutted, hydroelectric plants leveled.

And in a very real sense, the Korean War is still simmering. To this day—now for almost half a century since the cease-fire agreement—the United States has kept about 35,000 troops in South Korea as part of a Combined Forces Command to discourage any renewed North Korean aggression.

What had the Korean War accomplished? Historians, politicians, and millions of Americans affected forever by the war have asked that question. There are several answers. The Communist takeover of a country in Asia was stopped; South Korea survived as a non-Communist Republic of Korea. The United Nations passed its first test as an organization for collective world security. And, as President Clinton said, the collapse of the Soviet Union as a repressive world force almost certainly began with the failure of communism to win in South Korea.

A much more personal view of what was accomplished was expressed by James Brady, who was a twenty-three-year-old lieutenant in Korea. Now a journalist and the author of two Korean War books, Brady says about the war: "It did some positive things. It did save South Korea. It showed the Chinese that they were not invincible despite their millions and millions of men. We stopped them cold."

A MEMORIAL
FOR AMERICA'S
FORGOTTEN WAR

IT WAS NOT a forgotten war, of course. The almost two million men and women who served in the Korean War area would never forget it. The families of the nearly 150,000 men and women who were killed, wounded, or missing in the war would never forget it. They would always remember.

But the Korean War began in 1950, just five years after the end of World War II. That great war turned all of Europe, Asia, and the Pacific Islands into a battleground in which 16 million Americans fought and a million were killed or wounded. Americans had mobilized almost overnight for World War II and had supported the war

33

effort with courage and zeal because they knew the war threatened America's very existence. In 1945, World War II ended in a total victory for the United States and its allies.

Americans did not feel threatened by fighting in one small Asian country when it began in 1950. They were concerned with building homes, expanding factories for consumer goods, building new highways—all activities curtailed during World War II. The troubles in Korea were not a focus of national attention. President Truman downplayed the Korean War to the American public, always referring to it as a "police action" or a "conflict." The president did this because of his fear that the hostilities could explode into a third world war between the Communist giants, China and the Soviet Union, and the Western democracies. President Truman was determined not to let that happen.

The men and women who fought in World War II returned to hero welcomes. When Korean War veterans began returning home in the early 1950s, many Americans scarcely knew they had been away. Other Americans were puzzled by a war that had ended in a deadlock, a truce on a line almost exactly where it had started. And because Congress had not declared war in the Korea fighting, some organizations such as the Veterans of Foreign Wars would not grant membership to those who had fought in Korea.

As a result of such indifference and lack of understanding, Korean veterans quietly resumed their lives in America, and the Korean War faded into even greater obscurity. Were it not for some Vietnam War veterans, the sacrifices of the Korean veterans might have gone unsung.

Between 1965 and 1973 the United States fought another war in Asia, this time in the small Southeast Asian country of Vietnam. Again, the purpose of the U.S. effort was to prevent the spread of communism. This war was not fought under the flag of the United Nations; it was essentially an American war. Unlike the limited attention the Korean War received, Americans became intensely concerned about the war in Vietnam. The Vietnam War was America's first "television war." Day and night, month after month, year after year, national television brought the war into millions of American homes.

The Vietnam War sharply divided America. Millions of Americans felt that we had no business in Vietnam, that whether that country had a Communist or democratic government was an internal matter for the Vietnamese to decide. Millions of other Americans believed that a Communist Vietnam would lead to other Communist countries in Asia and the Pacific. American servicemen and -women returning from Vietnam were caught in the middle of the bitter dispute. Many veterans met with outright hostility.

In that climate of rejection, the idea of a Vietnam Veterans Memorial seemed unthinkable, even absurd. But to Jan Scruggs, a young veteran who had been wounded in Vietnam, it was neither unthinkable nor absurd. He became obsessed with the belief that America should have a memorial honoring its men and women who had served and died in Vietnam. Scruggs was convinced that such a memorial would help to heal the Vietnam War wounds that were still festering in America.

In an effort of total dedication beginning in 1979, Jan Scruggs and a small group of dedicated volunteers obtained congressional approval in 1980 for a Vietnam Veterans Memorial to be built on the Mall in Washington, DC. From private contributions, they raised the millions of dollars necessary to build it. A national competition for the memorial's design was won by a young Chinese-American architectural student named Maya Lin. Since its dedication in November 1982, the Vietnam Veterans Memorial has been acclaimed as one of the world's great war memorials. And it helped bring the healing to the nation that Jan Scruggs believed it would.

Probably motivated by Jan Scruggs's efforts, a few people began to advocate a Korean War Veterans Memorial as early as 1980. A bill to create such a memorial was introduced in Congress in 1982 but died in committee for lack of support. Without doubt, the dedication of the Vietnam Veterans Memorial in late 1982 triggered a grass-roots drive by Korean War veterans throughout the country for a memorial to those who fought and died in the earlier

Asian war. A new organization founded in 1984, the Korean War Veterans Association, gave a strong voice to the call for a memorial.

By 1985, Congress had become well aware that recognition of the valor of those who had fought in Korea was long overdue. A bill to authorize a Korean War Veterans Memorial was introduced in the House of Representatives by James Florio of New Jersey. The bill had 143 cosponsors. In the Senate the bill was introduced by William Lester Armstrong of Colorado and had strong support from John Chafee of Rhode Island, John Glenn of Ohio, Warren Rudman of New Hampshire, and John W. Warner of Virginia. All four were veterans of hard fighting in Korea.

The bill passed both houses of Congress overwhelmingly and was approved by President Ronald Reagan on October 28, 1986, as Public Law 99–572. The new law authorized the American Battle Monuments Commission—a small independent agency of the executive branch of the federal government—to build a Korean War Veterans Memorial to honor members of the U.S. Armed Forces who served in the Korean War. The memorial was to be built on government land in or near Washington, DC. The president was authorized to appoint a Korean War Veterans Memorial Advisory Board to recommend the site and design of the memorial and to encourage private donations to build the memorial. No government money was to be used.

President Reagan promptly appointed the Korean War Veterans Memorial Advisory Board, which from the beginning worked closely with the American Battle Monuments Commission to make the memorial a reality. The advisory board became the guiding spirit and driving force behind the memorial's creation.

All members of the advisory board had fought in the Korean War. The chairman was Retired General Richard G. Stilwell, who, as a colonel, had commanded an infantry regiment in two Korean War campaigns and, in his last duty assignment, in 1973, was commander in chief, United Nations Command; commander in chief, United States Forces in Korea; and commanding general, Eighth Army. The advisory board deputy chairman was Retired

General Raymond G. Davis of the U.S. Marine Corps, who was awarded the Congressional Medal of Honor for heroism in the Korean War.

In addition to Generals Stilwell and Davis, several advisory board members were retired military officers. One of those was Colonel Rosemary T. McCarthy, Army Nurse Corps. As a first lieutenant, she served in a surgical hospital in Korea. Among many other assignments, she was a camp nurse at Fort Wood in Japan during the occupation and served as a consultant on nursing to the surgeon general of the Army.

Of the original advisory board, no one exemplified the concept of service, courage, and sacrifice more clearly than Colonel William E. Weber. While serving in the 187th Airborne Regimental Combat Team, Weber—then a young captain—was severely wounded in a battle with Chinese forces near the 38th parallel in Korea. He lost both a leg and an arm. After almost two years of hospitalization and rehabilitation, he remained on active duty in the Army and built a distinguished career that included an assignment with the North Atlantic Treaty Organization (NATO) Command and several senior positions in the U.S. Department of Defense.

The advisory board's first task was to find the right site for the Korean War Veterans Memorial. The members agreed that it had to be in a highly visible location. "We didn't want an unseen memorial for a forgotten war," said Colonel Weber.

A site on Washington's tidal basin looking across at the Jefferson Memorial was an attractive possibility, but the advisory board strongly wanted their memorial to have a presence on the National Mall. One place available was a grassy, tree-filled area called Ash Woods at the western end of the Mall. The site was symbolically perfect: almost in the shadow of the Lincoln Memorial and just across the Mall's reflecting pool from the Vietnam Veterans Memorial.

But there was one serious problem. The Ash Woods area, like the entire west end of the Mall, is drained, reclaimed land, the product of a dredging and landfill program carried out by the U.S. Army Corps of Engineers late in the nineteenth century to fill in

A YOUNG MARINE *is fascinated by the steely combat patrol emerging from the shelter of the trees.*

the tidal flats of the Potomac River. A memorial on such unstable land would have to be supported by steel-reinforced concrete piers sunk to a bedrock depth of as much as 60 feet (18 meters). The Lincoln Memorial rests on 122 such piers. The design of the Korean War Veterans Memorial was not yet known, but without doubt there would be considerable weight. Such underpinning would add greatly to the cost. But the advisory board did not hesitate. Ash Woods was where the memorial should be, and the money would be found to build it there.

With the site selected, a national design competition for the Korean War Veterans Memorial was held, the instructions making clear the memorial's main purpose of honoring the men and women who fought in the Korean War. Instructions about where the memorial would be built and other necessary information were furnished to those entering the competition. The response from architects, artists, and landscape architects was excellent; more than five hundred entries were received. The advisory board spent months reviewing the entries, consulting with architects and memorial specialists.

In the spring of 1989 they announced their decision. The winning design was submitted by an architectural design team of faculty members from Pennsylvania State University. It featured a file of thirty-eight combat-clad soldiers advancing toward an American flag. The number of soldiers stood for the 38th parallel dividing North and South Korea; the figures would be made of gray Vermont granite. A black wall to one side of the soldiers would be filled with relief sculptures detailing the war.

An unveiling ceremony for the winning design was held in the Rose Garden of the White House on June 14, Flag Day. President George Bush told an audience of high-ranking veterans and their families that it was fitting on this day "to unveil the winning design of a symbol of liberty—the Korean War Veterans Memorial." Calling the Korean War "an American victory that remains too little appreciated and too little understood," President Bush continued, "today we say, 'No more'—it's time to remember."

With such a warm presidential launching, the Korean War Veterans Memorial seemed to be on its way to a smooth completion.

But Washington memorials have had a history of controversy. When its design was first announced, the Lincoln Memorial was criticized by many as "too grand" for the humble man it honored. The Washington Monument was a hundred years in its completion for a variety of reasons. Congress took more than twenty-five years to decide what kind of memorial Franklin D. Roosevelt should have. Some veterans groups at first had criticized the design of the Vietnam Veterans Memorial, calling it "a black gash of shame."

Soon the Korean War Veterans Memorial, too, found itself in the midst of controversy. While not wanting to glorify war, the advisory board did want more realism in the figures of the soldiers and some additional war action. They felt that the statues should be made of stainless steel rather than granite to enhance the realism.

All memorials built in Washington, DC, must be approved by two very powerful groups, the Commission of Fine Arts and the National Capital Planning Commission. Both commissions had serious doubts about the memorial design presented to them for approval by the Korean War Veterans Memorial Advisory Board and Cooper-Lecky Architects, a Washington firm that had been engaged to create the landscape design and oversee the building of the memorial.

The Commission of Fine Arts considered the design to be too big and unfocused, too much going on. The members wanted more "concentration and condensation." One member was concerned about the height and length of the wall. Another member felt that design changes showing some patrol figures being hit or responding to enemy fire were too melodramatic.

The controversy and the efforts of the advisory board and Cooper-Lecky to gain approval for the memorial's design continued through 1990 and 1991. The Pennsylvania State University team that had won the design competition withdrew from the project, unhappy with the many changes proposed for their original conception.

At last, however, in early 1992 an agreement was reached; the Commission of Fine Arts and the National Capital Planning Commission gave their approval. The number of figures would be reduced from thirty-eight to nineteen "to subdue their impact and better integrate them within the pastoral setting." Figures engaged in actual fighting would be eliminated. The background granite wall would be shortened by 55 feet (17 meters). Other changes in the landscape design were agreed on.

There would be a Korean War Veterans Memorial at last.

Despite the design problems, the advisory board had pushed forward with fund-raising efforts for the memorial. The law specified that construction could not begin until enough money had been raised to build it. Through raffles and other activities the Korean War Veterans Association was a major fund-raiser for the memorial and individual veterans groups contributed. For example, former members of Ranger units who fought in Korea sent repre-

THE PATROL *is moving toward an inscription that reads:*
OUR NATION HONORS HER SONS AND DAUGHTERS WHO ANSWERED
THE CALL TO DEFEND A COUNTRY THEY NEVER KNEW AND A PEOPLE
THEY NEVER MET.

sentatives to Washington to present a check for $11,000 for the memorial. The Treasury Department issued a silver dollar commemorating the Korean War; the coin sold for $30 and raised several million dollars for the memorial. American businesses also contributed a million dollars, and, in a show of sincere appreciation, South Korean businesses contributed more than twice that amount. By early 1992, the $18.1 million needed to build the memorial was in the bank.

On June 14, 1992, three years after the winning design was unveiled, President Bush spoke at the groundbreaking ceremony for the memorial. Many high-ranking military and government officials were at the ceremony in Ash Woods. But one was missing. General Richard G. Stilwell, who had served as advisory board chairman, was not there. He had died on Christmas Day, 1991. President Bush acknowledged General Stilwell's wife, Alice, and son Richard Jr., himself an Army lieutenant colonel, who were at the groundbreaking. Speaking of General Stilwell, the president said: "His dream is now about to come true, his leadership rewarded."

And then, speaking directly to the Korean War veterans in the audience, President Bush said: "I believe the Korean War showed that ours would not be the land of the free if it were not the home of the brave. And in that spirit, with eternal love for what you did and what you are, it is now my privilege to break the ground on behalf of every American for the Korean War Veterans Memorial."

4

THE FIGURES
AND MURAL WALL

THE MEMORIAL took three years to build. Sculptor

Frank C. Gaylord of Barre, Vermont, was chosen to create the fig-

ures of the nineteen servicemen in the patrol. In his first review of

the Korean War Veterans Memorial, Benjamin Forgey, *The Wash-*

ington Post's specialist on memorials, wrote this about Gaylord's

task: "It was an extraordinary challenge, one of the great figurative

assignments of the 20th century, and Gaylord came through."

Frank Gaylord is a career sculptor, whose larger-than-life stat-

uary is displayed throughout the nation. He served as a World War

II paratrooper with the 17th Airborne Division and fought in the

Battle of the Bulge in France. Gaylord sculpted some of the Korean War Veterans Memorial figures after real people, including a World War II friend whom he called his "foxhole buddy."

All branches of the services that fought in Korea are represented in the figures: Army, Air Force, Navy, Marines (the Marines

A MARINE CALLS *a warning to a comrade. The windblown panchos give a sense of movement and recall the harsh weather the troops endured for three years. "We knew that war through our feet," said one Korean War veteran. "We walked every inch of that country."*

have their helmet chin straps fastened at the insistence of the advisory board's Marine General Raymond Davis!). One of the figures is a South Korean "Katusa" (Korean Attached to United States Army). Racial and ethnic groups represented in the figures are white, twelve; African-American, three; Hispanic, two; Asian, one; American Indian, one.

"These are all combat people," Gaylord said about the figures. "They are people who got up in the morning and went into attack. They know what it's like."

Another statement by the sculptor helps to explain the intensely human quality in the faces of all the figures. Speaking of his own wartime experience, Gaylord said: "I can tell you the truth,

A SENSE OF DANGER *is etched in the soldier's face.*

the thing I needed most my first day in combat was my mother. I was frightened, and so was everybody else, but we functioned because we were trained."

Gaylord worked for several years on the combat patrol sculptures, starting before the final approval was given by the Commission of Fine Arts and the National Capital Planning Commission. He, advisory board members, and architect Kent Cooper spent wearisome days positioning full-scale fiberboard maquettes of the patrol figures in the Ash Woods memorial setting to determine their most effective arrangement. When cast in steel, the figures, all more than 7 feet tall (213 centimeters), would weigh approximately 1,000 pounds (454 kilograms) each. Concrete pilings or piers had to be sunk in the ground to support them before they arrived in Washington, and those preparations would take time.

The Tallix Art Foundry of Beacon, New York, cast Frank Gaylord's sculptures in stainless steel, giving them a dull gray cast. They were brought to Washington in three eighteen-wheeler trucks on April 17, 1995, and installed in their planned places in Ash Woods.

The memorial's mural wall is the work of Louis Nelson, a well-known New York industrial designer and graphic artist. His chief assistant in the huge project was Jennifer Stoller. The mural, which is 164 feet long (50 meters), contains more than 2,400 images from the Korean War. The wall is made of forty-one panels of highly polished Academy Black granite from California; the panels are 8 inches (20 centimeters) thick, and their total weight exceeds 100 tons (90.7 metric tons). The mural photographs were etched into the granite in Benday dots, a photoengraving process, at the Cold Spring Granite Company of Cold Spring, Minnesota.

Louis Nelson served in the Army in the early 1960s. "I came of age between the Korean and Vietnam War," he said, "and I served my country as a helicopter pilot in Germany when the [Berlin] Wall was being built in Berlin. Three decades later, when the Wall was dismantled, I started work on the design of the Korean Memorial. With it, a new wall arises—not one that divides, but one that will unite us."

MURAL ARTIST *Louis Nelson called the wall of photographs "the nation's mantelpiece."*

In making their selections for the mural, Nelson and Jennifer Stoller looked at 15,000 photographs from the National Archives and the Air and Space Museum. All of the equipment of war is portrayed in the black granite panels: rocket launcher, self-propelled gun, Patton tank, antiaircraft gun, hospital ship, many kinds of aircraft, and much, much more. But it is in the pictures of servicemen and -women that the mural wall truly comes alive.

The images—the tank crewman, the stretcher bearer, nurses, chaplains, pilots, surgeons, paratroopers, and many others—give the wall an almost haunting ghostly quality. The faces are Caucasian, African-American, Hispanic, Asian, American Indian.

About the wall, Louis Nelson said: "One way of commemorating service in the military, in the traditional sense, is to take a photograph of your loved one and put it on your mantelpiece. So I thought this would be nice to think of as the nation's mantelpiece."

THE REFLECTIVE POWER *of the wall increases the number of the combat patrol positioned only a stone's throw away from nineteen to thirty-eight.*

THE MURAL WALL *is endlessly fascinating for anyone with Korean War memories.*

The Korean War Veterans Memorial was dedicated on July 27, 1995. Thousands of Korean War veterans from all over the country came to the dedication.

In his dedication speech that day, President Bill Clinton summed up the significance of the newest memorial on the National Mall in one sentence: "It is a magnificent reminder of what is best about the United States."

5

WHAT THE KOREAN WAR VETERANS MEMORIAL SAYS TO AMERICA

AMERICA'S great memorials honor the deeds of its citizens who lived at important moments in the nation's history. The memorials are symbols that help define our national character. On the west end of Washington's Mall today stand three great war memorials. Each has a different message, but together they form a complementary, not a contradictory, threesome.

The Lincoln Memorial honors a great man who led the country out of a tragic Civil War and saved the Union. The memorial reminds us that great nations must have great leaders.

KOREAN WAR VETERANS *form the color guard at a ceremony on July 27, 2000, observing the 47ᵗʰ anniversary of the Korean War armistice.*

The Vietnam Veterans Memorial honors the men and women who fought and died in Vietnam; and its haunting back wall of names has a somber message for the nation: Any war, at any time and in any place, however necessary and for whatever moral purpose, is about sacrifice and sorrow, not about glory and reward.

The Korean War Veterans Memorial does many things. It honors the service and sacrifice of almost two million Americans who fought a savage war to halt communist aggression.

It reminds us that, for the first time in history, a world organization of nations came together to oppose aggression and succeeded, largely because of the valor of American fighting forces.

The memorial does not glorify war, but it reminds us that patriotism and the willingness to serve in a citizens' army in times of national crisis lie at the heart of our democracy.

YOU CANNOT PASS *the mural wall without becoming part of it.*

A SPECIAL VETERAN'S DAY *picture for a group of Korean War veterans.*

More than anything else, the Korean War Veterans Memorial tells us that freedom is not free, that the price of freedom is constant vigilance, the willingness to sacrifice, and the readiness to come together in a total national effort to fight tyranny.

At the dedication ceremony for the Korean War Veterans Memorial, President Clinton said: ". . . in steel and granite, water and earth, the creators of this memorial have brought to life the courage and sacrifice of those who served in all branches of the Armed Forces from every racial and ethnic group and background in America. They represent, once more, the enduring American truth: From many we are one."

INFORMATION
ABOUT THE
KOREAN WAR
VETERANS
MEMORIAL

THE KOREAN WAR VETERANS MEMORIAL is

staffed from 8:00 A.M. to midnight every day except December 25

by park rangers who are available to answer questions and give talks

about the memorial.

HONOR ROLL: In the National Park Service kiosk located

near the memorial is a bank of computers listing the names of all

those who died in the Korean War as well as those still listed as

missing in action and those captured as prisoners during the war.

Photographs of those listed, supplied by families and friends, are

shown on the computers.

MEMORIAL WEB SITE ADDRESS:

www.nps.gov/kwvm

Additional information about the Korean War Veterans Memorial can be obtained by contacting the National Park Service as specified below:

Superintendent
National Capital Parks-Central
900 Ohio Drive, SW
Washington, DC 20024

Telephone: (202) 485–9880

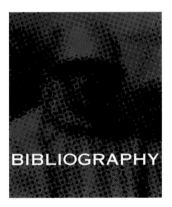

BIBLIOGRAPHY

"An Overview of the U.S. Army in the Korean War" (Fact Sheet), Army Center of Military History, Washington, DC, 2000.

Ashabranner, Brent. *Their Names to Live: What the Vietnam Veterans Memorial Means to America*. Brookfield, CT: Twenty-First Century Books, 1998.

Brady, James. "'He Was the Most Admirable Man I've Ever Known'," *Parade* magazine, June 25, 2000. (About Korean War hero John Chafee.)

———. *The Marine of Autumn*. New York: St. Martin's Press, 2000.

"Brief History of the Marine Corps in the Korean War" (Fact Sheet), Marine Corps History and Museums Division: Washington, DC, 2000.

Cumings, Bruce. *Korea's Place in the Sun*. New York: W. W. Norton & Company, 1997.

Facts about Korea. Seoul: Korean Overseas Information Service, 1993.

Forgey, Benjamin. "The March of Peace: Moving Memorial to Korea Veterans Surpasses the Tortured History of Its Design," *The Washington Post*, July 22, 1995.

Kilian, Michael. "Forgotten War Remembered 42 Years Later: A D.C. Memorial Will Honor Veterans of Korea," *Chicago Tribune*, July 27, 1995.

McCullough, David. *Truman*. New York: Simon & Schuster, 1992.

Millet, Allan R. "A Reader's Guide to the Korean War," *The Journal of Military History*, July 1997.

"Naval Operations During the Korean War" (Fact Sheet), The Naval Historical Center, Washington, DC, 2000.

Stokesbury, James L. *A Short History of the Korean War*. New York: William Morrow & Company, 1988.

"The United States Air Force in the Korean War" (Fact Sheet), Office of the Air Force Historian, Washington, DC, 2000.

Vogel, Steve. "Two Heroes Honored in the Breach," *The Washington Post*, May 28, 2000.

———. "Unprepared to Fight," *The Washington Post*, June 19, 2000.

Vogel, Steve, and William Branigin. "The War They Can't Forget," *The Washington Post*, June 26, 2000.

Wheeler, Linda. "Korean War Memorial Marks New Beginning," *The Washington Post*, June 28, 1999.

Williams, Rudy. "Memorial Reminds That 'Freedom Is Not Free'," American Forces Press Service, June 21, 2000.

A KOREAN WAR

CHRONOLOGY

JUNE 25: Armed forces of the Democratic People's Republic of Korea (North Korea) cross the 38th parallel, invading the Republic of Korea (South Korea). The United Nations (UN) adopts a resolution calling for North Korean forces to withdraw to north of 38th parallel.

JUNE 27: President Harry S Truman approves U.S. air and naval assistance for South Korea. United Nations asks member countries to help South Korea.

JUNE 29: North Korean forces capture Seoul, capital of South Korea.

JUNE 30: President Truman orders U.S. ground forces to Korea.

JULY 5: Near city of Osan, U.S. forces retreat with heavy losses in first battle with North Korean army.

JULY 7: General Douglas MacArthur appointed supreme commander of UN forces in Korea.

JULY 22: U.S. troops retreat from temporary South Korean capital of Taejon after days of fighting.

AUGUST 27–SEPTEMBER 15: In some of war's bitterest fighting, UN forces stop North Korean advance at Pusan perimeter.

SEPTEMBER 15: General MacArthur orders amphibious assault landing at Inchon near Seoul.

SEPTEMBER 19–29: UN troops battle North Korean forces and recapture Seoul.

OCTOBER 9: UN authorizes its forces to cross 38th parallel into North Korea to restore peace and security.

OCTOBER 19: Pyongyang, North Korean capital, captured by UN forces.

OCTOBER 25: Communist China enters war. Massive Chinese armies cross Yalu River border into North Korea, forcing UN troops to retreat.

NOVEMBER 27: Eight Chinese divisions trap U.S. Marines and other UN forces at Changjin (Chosin) Reservoir. UN forces fight way to safety in one of war's longest engagements.

DECEMBER 1–24: Chinese and North Korean armies force UN troops to retreat on all fronts.

DECEMBER 25: Northern forces recross 38th parallel as Communist offensive returns to South Korea.

1951

JANUARY 4: UN forces evacuate Seoul, which again falls to Northern Communists.

JANUARY–FEBRUARY: UN forces fight back, begin Operations Thunderbolt, Killer, Ripper.

MARCH 15: UN forces recapture Seoul.

JULY 10: Truce talks begin at Kaesong but fighting continues.

AUGUST–OCTOBER: Battles of Bloody Ridge and Heartbreak Ridge.

1952

APRIL 18: Communist negotiators refuse to allow voluntary repatriation of prisoners.

OCTOBER 8: Truce talks broken off.

1953

MARCH–APRIL: Fighting continues, Battles of Old Baldy and Pork Chop Hill.

MARCH 28: UN proposes exchange of sick and wounded prisoners. Communists accept.

APRIL 26: Truce talks resume.

JULY 27: Armistice agreement signed at Panmunjom. Fighting stops.

INDEX

Page numbers in *italics* refer to illustrations.